LIFE'S LITTLE
TREASURE BOOK

On
Mothers

H. JACKSON BROWN, JR.

RUTLEDGE HILL PRESS®

NASHVILLE, TENNESSEE

Published in Nashville, Tennessee, by Rutledge Hill Press, Inc., 211 Seventh Avenue North, Nashville, Tennessee 37219. Distributed in Canada by H. B. Fenn and Co., Ltd., 34 Nixon Road, Bolton, Ontario L7E 1W2. Distributed in Australia by The Five Mile Press Pty., Ltd., 22 Summit Road, Noble Park, Victoria 3174. Distributed in New Zealand by Tandem Press, 2 Rugby Road, Birkenhead, Auckland 10. Distributed in the United Kingdom by Verulam Publishing, Ltd., 152a Park Street Lane, Park Street, St. Albans, Hertfordshire AL2 2AU.

Typography by Compass Communications, Inc., Nashville, Tennessee

Illustrations by Sandra Roberts

Book design by Harriette Bateman

ISBN: 1-55853-609-4

Printed in Mexico

1 2 3 4 5 6 7 8 9—02 01 00 99 98

INTRODUCTION

*T*here is no love like a mother's love. Hers is the first voice heard, the first face seen, and the first tender touch we know. No one loves us as devotedly and is willing to forgive us so completely.

As lifegiver, caretaker, teacher, adviser, heroine, and friend, our mothers exert an unparalleled influence on our destiny. No one has a greater effect on what we become or on how far we'll go.

Abraham Lincoln wrote, "All that I am or hope to be I owe to my angel mother." Many of us feel the same way. When asked about their mothers' influence, college students had this to say. "She always believed in me." "Stood by me through it all." "Understands me better than I do myself." "Taught me through her excellent example." "Made sacrifices for me that I'll never be able to repay."

The sacrifices made by mothers are profound and legendary; and to those of us who receive them, beyond reparation. For no matter how often and fervently we try to repay them, the scales still tilt in our mothers' favor.

With that in mind, I offer this collection as a contribution to the debt I owe my own mother, Sarah. It is a small and imperfect offering, but one inspired by my deepest feelings of gratitude and love.

God could not be everywhere and therefore He made mothers.

—Jewish Proverb

Motherhood is like planting sequoia trees. You have to wait a long time to find out how you've done.

—HJB

*I*f I had listened to my mom, I would have avoided 90 percent of life's problems.

—Age 20

❧

*I*t's hard to lie when you are looking into your mom's eyes.

—Age 9

$\mathcal{N}$othing makes me happier
than hearing my three-year-
old say, "You're the best mom
ever and I love you."

—Age 31

∾

$\mathcal{M}$y dad could always get my
mom to smile with these
three words, "Let's eat out."

—Age 41

There's no greater resource
when you're a new mother
than your own mother.

—Age 29

❧

Example is not the main
thing in life—it is the
only thing.

—Albert Schweitzer

Favorite quote of Howard Clark's mother, Brenda

I looked on child rearing not only as a work of love and duty but as a profession that was fully as interesting and challenging as any honorable profession in the world and one that demanded the best that I could bring to it.

— Rose Kennedy

*T*hough we travel the world
over to find the beautiful,
we must carry it with us or we
find it not.

—Ralph Waldo Emerson

Favorite quote of Pamela Martin's mother, Barbara

❧

*I*f mom's on a diet, everyone's
on a diet.

—Age 10

At the birth of her first child, a woman becomes a mother— something totally different from what she was just moments before.

$\mathcal{W}$hen your mother is mad and asks you, "Do I look stupid?" it's best not to answer her.

—Age 13

∾

$\mathcal{M}$y daughter's best qualities are the same as my mother's.

—Age 21

Cleaning your house while
your kids are still growing
Is like shoveling the walk
before it stops snowing.

—Phyllis Diller

Mom used to say . . .

- Remember that calamine lotion, warm oatmeal and hugs will cure about anything.

- Never buy an article of clothing thinking it will fit if you lose a couple of pounds.

- Whenever you hear an ambulance siren, say a prayer for the person inside.

- Hold puppies, kittens and babies any chance you get.

- Don't wait for someone else to make your life terrific. That's your job.

Treat people as if they were what they ought to be and you help them to become what they are capable of being.

—Johann Wolfgang von Goethe

Favorite quote of Sophia Earthman's mother, Nettie

Stories first heard at a
mother's knee are never
wholly forgotten—a little
spring that never quite dries
up in our journey through
scorching years.

—Giovanni Ruffini

Mother is the name of God in
the lips and hearts of children.

—William Makepeace Thackery

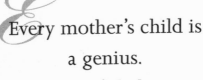

Every mother's child is
a genius.
If you don't believe it,
just ask her.

$\mathcal{F}$or the faithful in married love, there is no one to envy and in each other's love, wealth beyond measure.

—Unknown

Favorite quote of Karen Strain's mother, Joyce

$\mathcal{B}$e scared, but act courageously.

—motherly advice to Judith Silinsky

My mother was the making of me. She was so true, so sure of me, and I felt that I had someone to live for; someone I must not disappoint.

—Thomas Edison

No matter how tempting a bowl of ice cream, a slice of cheesecake, or even chocolate seems, my mother only has to say one word before I put it all back: **bi-ki-ni**.

—Age 18

You know you're in real trouble when your mom calls you by both your first and middle names.

—Age 9

All that I am, or hope to be,
I owe to my angel mother.

—Abraham Lincoln

❧

No joy in nature is so
sublimely affecting as the joy
of a mother at the good fortune
of her child.

—Jean Paul Richter

*W*aiting until you are married to have sex is the best advice my mother ever gave me and a treasure I cherish with my husband. It makes me feel secure, especially since his mother gave him the same advice and he followed it too.

—Age 27

$\mathcal{M}$oms have a tender heart, loving arms, a patient smile, and are one hundred times more sensitive than a radar tracking device.

—Age 11

&

$\mathcal{M}$y day is perfect when a song comes on the radio and my one-year-old wants to dance with me.

—Age 21

Being told that I am just like my mother is the best compliment I've ever been given.

—Age 21

My mother was an angel on earth. She was a minister of blessings to all human beings within her sphere of action. Her heart was the abode of heavenly purity. She had no feelings but of kindness and beneficence, yet her mind was as firm as her temper was mild and gentle.

—John Quincy Adams

No matter how closely
I follow her recipe,
my cooking never tastes as
good as my mom's.

—Age 24

∾

No one will ever engrave
"She kept a tidy house" on a
mother's tombstone.

—Susan Causdale

Every mother is like
Moses. She does not
enter the promised
land. She prepares a
world she will
never see.

—Pope Paul VI

When God thought of mother,
He must have laughed with
satisfaction and framed it
quickly — so rich, so deep, so
divine, so full of soul, power and
beauty was the conception.

—Henry Ward Beecher

*Who ran to help me when
I fell,
And would some pretty
story tell,
Or kiss the place to make
it well?
My Mother.*

—Ann Taylor,
from the poem "My Mother"

If mom says no, she means it. If dad says no, it means maybe.

—Age 13

You can't pretend you're sick and expect your mom to let you go to the mall.

—Age 14

Children, look in those eyes,
listen to that dear voice, notice
the feeling of even a single
touch that is bestowed upon
you by that gentle hand.
Make much of it while yet
you have the most precious of
all good gifts, a loving
mother. In after life you

*may have friends, fond, dear
friends, but never will you
have again the inexpressible
love and gentleness lavished
upon you, which none but a
mother bestows.*

—Thomas Babington Macaulay

My mom used to say that there are two ways of spreading light: to be the candle or to be the mirror that reflects it.

—Age 47

*N*ever throw a tantrum at
the same time your child is
throwing one.

—Age 31

❧

*A*s a mom, I have more
important things to worry
about than which parts of my
body are getting closer
to the ground.

—Age 59

It's a
mother's job
to nag.

—Age 9

*The mother . . . holds the key
of the soul; and it is she who
stamps the coin of character.*

—Unknown

❧

*Nature's loving proxy, the
watchful mother*

—Edward Bulver

They always looked back before turning the corner, for their mother was always at the window to nod and smile, and wave her hand at them. Somehow it seemed as if they couldn't have got through the day without that, for whatever their mood might be, the last glimpse of that motherly face was sure to affect them like sunshine.

—Louisa May Alcott

When your children become adults, they always want the recipes for the meals they used to hide in their napkins and feed to the dog.

—Age 21

∾

When my mother would give me that LOOK, I'd turn into Little Miss Perfect.

—Age 30

$\mathcal{T}$here is no greater joy than in knowing all my children are safe, asleep in their beds, and happy and proud that I'm their mom.

—Age 34

∞

$\mathcal{M}$y mom will always take my side in an argument as long as it is not with her.

—Age 37

*In the sheltered simplicity
of the first days after a baby is
born, one sees again the
magical closed circle, the
miraculous sense of two people
existing only for each other.*

—Anne Morrow Lindbergh

*R*egardless of my
accomplishments, my mother
is constantly looking for signs
of improvement.

—Age 32

∾

*T*he easiest way to get
grounded is to interrupt my
mother during *Seinfeld*.

—Age 17

$\mathcal{M}$oms are too busy to
get sick.

—Age 31

∾

$\mathcal{W}$hen I was learning how
to drive, my mom would
often use the invisible brake
on her side of the car.

—Age 22

An ounce of mother
is worth
a pound of clergy.

—Spanish Proverb

*She watches over the ways of
her household,
And does not eat the bread of
idleness.
Her children rise up and call
her blessed;
Her husband also, and he
praises her.*

—Proverbs 31:27–28

My mother was the most beautiful woman I ever saw. All I am I owe to my mother. I attribute all my successes in life to the moral, intellectual, and physical education I received from her.

—George Washington

$\mathcal{W}$e can do anything we want,
if we stick to it long enough.

—Helen Keller

Favorite quote of Lucy Ashmore's mother, Delores

$\mathcal{T}$he first great gift we can
bestow on others is a
good example.

—Sir Charles Morell

Favorite quote of Pete Sherlock's mother, Jill

A mother's love endures through it all; in good repute, in bad repute, in the face of the world's condemnation.

—Washington Irving

∾

When my teenagers had a problem, I found the best way to discuss it was over a pint of Ben & Jerry's.

—Age 59

The best thing to give your enemy is forgiveness; to an opponent, tolerance; to a fiancée, your heart; to your child, a good example; to a father, deference; to your mother, conduct that will make her proud of you; to yourself, respect; to all men, charity.

—Arthur James Balfour

A mom who
can potty train
triplets
can do anything.

—Age 29

*I*t's important to be my daughter's friend, but it's more important to be her mother.

—Age 35

∾

*N*o matter how old I get, I like my mom taking care of me when I'm sick.

—Age 25

If your mom is asleep,
don't wake her up.

—Age 10

∾

A mother never quite leaves
her children at home,
even when she doesn't take
them along.

—Age 62

*T*hose who bring sunshine to the lives of others cannot help but keep it for themselves.

—James M. Barrie

Favorite quote of Seth Boykin's mother, Elizabeth

∽

*I*n the long run, you hit only what you aim at. Therefore, though you should fail immediately, you had better aim at something high.

—Henry David Thoreau

Favorite quote of Joel Stricker's mother, Bonnie

A mother is the truest friend we have, when trials heavy and sudden fall upon us; when adversity takes the place of prosperity; when friends who rejoice with us in our sunshine desert us; when troubles thicken around us;

still will she cling to us, and
endeavor by her kind
precepts and counsels to
dissipate the clouds of
darkness, and cause peace to
return to our hearts.

—Washington Irving

Mother: That was the bank where we deposited all our hurt and worries.

—T. DeWitt Talmage

❧

Men are what their mothers made them.

—Ralph Waldo Emerson

*W*henever I'm singing a
lullaby to my six-month-old
son, I hear my mother's voice
and I am comforted.

—Age 26

∾

*T*he most powerful thing
a mom can say is,
"I forgive you."

—Kris Tommensen

All women become like their mothers. That is their tragedy. No man does. That is his.

—Oscar Wilde

∾

Even though mother died many years ago, whenever something wonderful happens to me, my first reaction still is, "I can't wait to tell Mom."

—Age 48

*My mother was the source
from which I derived the
guiding principles of life.*

—John Wesley

❧

*Of all the rights of women, the
greatest is to be a mother.*

—Lin Yutang

I know I'm in for a long
lecture when my mom
begins with, "When I was
your age. . . ."

—Age 11

❧

If your mother made
pimento cheese with Miracle
Whip, you don't like it when
it's made with mayonnaise.

—Age 32

Youth fades; love droops;
the leaves of
friendship fall;
A mother's secret love
outlives them all.

—Oliver Wendell Holmes

There is religion in all deep love, but the love of a mother is the veil of a softer light, between the heart and the heavenly father.

—Samuel Taylor Coleridge

Motherhood: It's the biggest on-the-job training program in existence today.

—Erma Bombeck

He who receives a benefit
should never forget it; he
who bestows should never
remember it.

—Pierre Charron

Favorite quote of Travis Maddox's mother, Monique

❧

The art of being wise is
the art of knowing what
to overlook.

—William James

Favorite quote of Pat Woody's mother, Julia

The last day of school before summer vacation is the shortest day of a mother's year.

—Dee Eldridge

❧

The trouble with being a parent is that by the time ~~~~ experienced, ~~~~ employed.

—Rosemary Coleton

—Age 39

As a Mom,
I've learned that . . .

. . . I should never buy white T-shirts for boys under thirteen.

—Age 43

. . . when you greet your children each morning with a smile and a hug, it starts their day out right and your day too.

. . . I can't sleep until all my children are in for the night.

—Age 47

. . . there is nothing more painful to witness than grieving parents.

—Age 47

. . . children need loving the most when they are the hardest to love. —Age 79

*M*y mom has eyes in the back of her head.

—Age 6

❧

*T*here's no place in our house where my mom can't hear me.

—Age 8

No longer forward or behind
I look in hope or fear;
But grateful, take the good I find,
The best of now and here.

—John Greenleaf Whittier

Favorite quote of Hailey Myers's mother, Lydia

A man loves his sweetheart
the most, his wife the best,
but his mother the longest.

—Irish Proverb

The future destiny of
the child is always the work
of the mother.

—Napoleon

Mother, you wrote no lofty
    poems that critics consider
    art;
But with a nobler vision, you
    lived them in your heart.
    —Thomas Fessenden

$\mathcal{N}$othing has spoken more
loudly to me than my
mother's quiet example.

—Age 41

∾

$\mathcal{T}$he moment my pregnancy
test was positive, I became
my mother.

—Age 21

If you would reform the world from its errors and vices, begin by enlisting the mothers

—Charles Simmons

❧

The babe at first feeds upon the mother's bosom, but is always on her heart.

—Henry Ward Beecher

Some are kissing mothers and some are scolding mothers, but it is love just the same, and most mothers kiss and scold together.

—Pearl S. Buck

❧

A rich child often sits in a poor mother's lap.

—Danish Proverb

My mother had a slender, small body, but a large heart — a heart so large that everybody's grief and everybody's joy found welcome in it, and hospitable accommodation.

—Mark Twain

Remember that when
your mom says,
"you'll regret it,"
you usually will.

A mother who is really a mother, is never free.

—Honoré de Balzac

The mother's heart is the child's schoolroom.

—Henry Ward Beecher

$\mathcal{M}$om used to say that life
doesn't have to be perfect to
be wonderful.

—Age 50

❧

$\mathcal{Y}$ou only have one mom
and you should take good
care of her.

—Age 12

No language can express the power and beauty and heroism and majesty of a mother's love. It shrinks not where man cowers, and grows stronger where man faints, and over the wastes of worldly fortune sends the radiance of its quenchless fidelity like a star in heaven.

—Edwin Chapin

$\mathcal{M}$y kids can con me into
doing things for them by
saying, "But it's so much
better when you do it, Mom."

—Age 33

❧

$\mathcal{N}$o matter how much your
children love you, you can't
compete with candy.

—Age 21

*D*espite all the loving
and caring relationships in
the world, there is nothing
more loving than my
mother's hand on my
forehead when I am sick.

—Age 17

∽

*Y*ou shouldn't bug a
pregnant mom.

—Age 11

Oh, to be only half as wonderful as my child thought I was when he was small, and only half as stupid as my teenager now thinks I am.

—Rebecca Richards

There is only one pretty child in the world, and every mother has it.

—Chinese Proverb

❧

Who takes the child by the hand takes the mother by the heart.

—Danish Proverb

The time to be happy is now; the place to be happy is here; the way to be happy is to make others so.

—Robert Green Ingersoll

Favorite quote of Ginger Kerr's mother, Margaret

*C*hildren are what the
mothers are; no father's
fondest care can so fashion
the infant's heart, or so shape
the life.

—Walter Savage Landor

Favorite quote of Leah Sears's mother, Rachael

❧

*I*f I asked if there ever
existed any perfect moms,
most would say, only one;
then proudly mention
their own.

Act as if your mother
is right behind you,
because someone's
mother always is.